HOW DID THEY BUILD THAT?

HOW DID THEY BUILD THAT?

AIRPORT

BY MATT MULLINS

COMMUNITY · CONNECTIONS ?

Published in the United States of America by Cherry Lake Publishing
Ann Arbor, Michigan
www.cherrylakepublishing.com

Content Adviser: Nancy Kristof
Reading Adviser: Cecilia Minden-Cupp, PhD, Literacy Consultant

Photo Credits: Cover and page 1, ©yxm2008, used under license from Shutterstock, Inc.;
page 5, ©Ramon Berk, used under license from Shutterstock, Inc.; page 7, ©Taylor Jackson,
used under license from Shutterstock, Inc.; page 9, ©Poco_bw/Dreamstime.com; page 11,
©Charles Polidano/Touch The Skies/Alamy; page 13, ©Stephen Coburn, used under license
from Shutterstock, Inc.; page 15, ©Darryl Brooks, used under license from Shutterstock, Inc.;
page 17, ©Lisa F. Young, used under license from Shutterstock, Inc.; page 19, ©James Steidl,
used under license from Shutterstock, Inc.; page 21, ©Robert Quinlan/Alamy.

LIBRARY OF CONGRESS CATALOGING-IN-PUBLICATION DATA
Mullins, Matt.
  How did they build that? Airport / by Matt Mullins.
    p. cm.—(Community connections)
  Includes index.
  ISBN-13: 978-1-60279-486-3
  ISBN-10: 1-60279-486-3
  1. Airport buildings—Juvenile literature. 2. Airports —Juvenile literature. I. Title. II. Series.
  TL725.15.M85 2010
  690'.539—dc22   2008046142

Cherry Lake Publishing would like to acknowledge the
work of The Partnership for 21st Century Skills. Please
visit www.21stcenturyskills.org for more information.

AIRPORT

CONTENTS

APR 1 7 2010

HOW DID THEY BUILD THAT?

AT THE AIRPORT

Airports can be big or small. At some airports, giant jet planes zoom in. Hundreds of people walk off the planes. Hundreds more walk on and zoom away.

At other airports, small planes glide in. Sometimes only one person walks out of the plane.

An airport's size can depend on the size of the planes that will land there.

Have you ever been to an airport? Did you see the runway? It's like a long street where planes take off and land. Maybe you saw the air traffic control tower. That is where men and women direct airplane traffic.

The air traffic control tower has many windows. This allows the people who control air traffic to see the planes that are moving.

7

Maybe you were in the **terminal**. People can buy airplane tickets in the terminal. It is also where people get on and off airplanes.

Hangars are like garages for airplanes. Airplanes are often repaired inside them.

LOOK!

Look around when you get to the airport. What buildings can you see? Many airports have giant metal sheds called **hangars**. Some hangars are square. Others look like big, metal half circles called domes.

MAKING A PLAN

The **airport authority** is a group of people in charge of an airport. They decide how big it should be. They think about how many people will use the airport. They figure out how many planes will fly in and out.

A busy airport needs terminals that can hold many people.

11

Architects design buildings. Some help **design** airports. Architects help decide what the airport will look like.

Engineers build large **structures**. They work with the architects. They help figure out how long and wide to make the runways. They help decide the size of the terminal.

Architects and engineers look at detailed plans called blueprints. The blueprints are the instructions for building an airport or other building.

13

BUILD IT

Building begins when the design is ready. First, workers clear the land. They use machines to make the ground flat. Then they use concrete to make smooth runways. They build the terminal and the control tower. They make floors and walls.

It takes many workers and machines to build a new airport.

Electricians run wires through walls and floors. They bring power to lights and machines. Plumbers connect sinks and toilets to pipes. The pipes carry fresh water in and dirty water out. Some workers build counters. Others put carpet in place.

Electricians and other construction workers follow many safety rules. Their work can be dangerous if they are not careful.

Do you know any engineers or architects? How about electricians or plumbers? If you do, ask them about their jobs. Find out how they do their work. Asking questions can help you learn more about how structures are built.

17

Other **contractors** work on things found only in airports. Some install computers to track when planes take off and land. Some work on security systems to keep travelers safe. Others help with baggage systems to keep suitcases moving.

All of this work takes time. It can take 10 years to plan and build a large airport.

Special security systems are built in airports. They help keep travelers and airport workers safe.

A BUSY PLACE

A big airport is like a small city. It takes many people to build one. After it is built, thousands of people pass through the airport each day. Some work there. Others travel on planes. There are few places busier than an airport!

It takes a lot of land to build an airport!

THINK!

Many airports have their own fire stations. Many also have their own hotels. Can you think of some other buildings you might find in a large airport?

21

GLOSSARY

airport authority (AIR-port uh-THOR-uh-tee) a group of people in charge of making decisions about an airport

architects (AR-ki-tektss) people who design buildings and other large structures

contractors (KON-track-turz) people or companies that build a specific structure

design (di-ZINE) to create a detailed drawing and plan for construction

electricians (i-lek-TRISH-uhnz) people who install, maintain, or repair electrical wiring and equipment

engineers (en-juh-NIHRZ) people trained to design and build structures

hangars (HANG-urz) shelters for aircraft

structures (STRUHK-shurz) things that have been built, such as large buildings, dams, or bridges

terminal (TUR-muh-nuhl) a building at which an air journey begins and ends

FIND OUT MORE

BOOKS

Hutchings, Amy. *What Happens at an Airport?* Pleasantville, NY: Weekly Reader Pub., 2009.

Masters, Nancy Robinson. *Airplanes*. Ann Arbor: Cherry Lake Publishing, 2008.

WEB SITES

Federal Aviation Administration Kid's Corner
www.faa.gov/education/student_resources/kids_corner/
Coloring books, puzzles, and more information about air travel

Metropolitan Washington Airports Authority—Kids Page
www.metwashairports.com/kids/kids_page
Links to information about airport construction, travel safety, airport history, and more

23

INDEX

ABOUT THE AUTHOR

Matt Mullins lives
with his wife and
son in Madison,
Wisconsin. Formerly
a journalist, Matt
writes about science
and engineering,
current affairs,
food and wine, and
anything else that
draws his interest.